Essays on Order, Book 4

The Fourth Collection of Essays

    Book 1 consisted of essays designed to engage the reader in self-awareness and an awareness of the order and chaos that surrounds us all. Book 2 was to take the reader one step deeper into what order can do and what chaos cannot, revelation. Book 3 took the reader to the next step of order, understanding. Book 4 will assist the reader in knowing order and seeing when and where chaos is being applied.

    As in the first three books, you should try not to read all the essays in a single reading. I suggest you read one essay, think about it, re-read it, and then re-think it before moving to the next essay. In this manner you will absorb more of the idea than just the content. This is simply an ordered approach for you to read the Essays on Order, good luck and enjoy the essays.

www.essaysonorder.com

Chuck Pyburn

Essays on Order

The Fourth Collection of Essays

Book 4 – Table of Contents

1. An Essay on Order – A Belief in People
2. An Essay on Order – Mirrors Lie
3. An Essay on Order – The Age of Alphas
4. An Essay on Order – Predestination
5. An Essay on Order – Homeostasis, The Balance of Life
6. An Essay on Order – The Fallen Thought
7. An Essay on Order – Friendship
8. An Essay on Order – Rituals
9. An Essay on Order – The Classes
10. An Essay on Order – Arming a Population
11. An Essay on Order – Acceptance
12. An Essay on Order – Melancholy
13. An Essay on Order – Proof
14. An Essay on Order – Power and the Population
15. An Essay on Order – Poverty
16. An Essay on Order – Dominance
17. An Essay on Order – Reckoning
18. An Essay on Order – Change
19. An Essay on Order – Peace
20. An Essay on Order – The Final Essay

An Essay on Order – A Belief in People

Somewhere around eight years old I used to hang out at the local bike shop. All I was good for was fetching tools and pretty much just being a pain in the ass but the mechanics seemed to tolerate me. One Friday they invited me with them for some after work supper at the Pig Diner and yes that was the name of it. During the burgers the subject of a belief in people came up and I asked the question, "What is a belief in people?" The answer I got along with a lot of soul searching produced this essay.

The Essay

A belief in people dates back to the first father and mother having their first child. As the parents look at their baby all they can see is hard work and sacrifice in their future. By sheer determination, the parents have decided that the child's life will be easier than theirs. With each passing generation these thoughts and wishes are passed until the population of today is in control.

Looking back through time is easy enough; populations have endured natural catastrophes, enslavement, being a conquered people and at times freedom. Regardless of the circumstance, the populations have strove to embetter their lot with each passing generation. In days of old this embetterment took centuries but with the passing of time and the advancement of technology an embettered society occurs in years, one step at a time. A belief in people does not require the benevolence of government nor does it require the permission of religion, it only requires the parental love of a child.

This is not to say that every child will have it better than their parents, it is only to say that the belief in people will always exists so long as men walk the earth. Order requires this belief and without it there would surely be chaos.

Chuck Pyburn

An Essay on Order – Mirrors Lie

Growing up looking different and then constantly being harassed about looking different, you develop a perception regarding looks. It seemed like fitting in required looking like the other folks, dressing like the other folks and then having the same attitude as the other folks. As I grew my resentment grew until I was big enough to physically fight back. As a child I thought I could fight my way into the group, no such luck. The only real way to 'fight back' is to know what you are looking at, enjoy the essay.

The Essay

Being able to see one's reflection in a pool of water has existed since the beginning. Actual mirrored surfaces were not created until around 600 BC and finally what is currently regarded as a mirror was not invented until around the 1400's. It wasn't until the early 1700's that mirrors started to become available to the less affluent members of the population. And finally today, mirrors are as common as shoes. What has never changed in regards to a reflection is the purpose of seeing that reflection.

The reflection one sees in a mirror displays the outward appearance of an individual. This appearance is staged to allow the person to interact within the population. The appearance does not reflect the individual's past or future but reflects only what the individual is seeking today. The one aspect of an individual that is not reflected in the mirror is the person's psyche. An individual's appearance and psyche are never one and the same. Whereas one's appearance is static, an individual's psyche is dynamic in that it constantly adapting to one's circumstance, the population and the environment and all the while maintaining a focus on that which is sought. These conditions are reoccurring on a daily basis within the entire population and as such are based on order so long as that which is sought is also based on order. If it is the case that what is sought is not based on order then the conditions become an exercise in chaos. This chaos will exist for that member, or those members, of the population that are engaged in seeking this acquisition.

It then becomes incumbent on those members of the population that engage these members of the population to recognize the existence of these conditions as the interaction occurs. One should recognize that appearance alone will not reveal the acquisition that is sought after by an engaging member, or members, of a population. Knowing what is sought after will only be revealed over time as the interaction escalates through verbal and written communication and demonstrated actions.

      While the aforementioned conditions are true for an individual, they are equally true for populations. It will never be the case that an individual, or population, can display their true intentions regarding the acquisition they seek. It will always be the case that an individual's, or population's, appearance may be tailored to present any manner of intention or lack of intention as the interaction is engaged. For the ordered the mandate is clear, mirrors lie.

Chuck Pyburn

An Essay on Order – The Age of Alphas

One of things I always wondered about was how girls and boys got together. I never had much luck with the babes but like any guy I was always interested and looking. After about a hundred years or so of thinking about it this essay came to mind.

The Essay

If one were to step back in history before there were nations, before there were empires, before there were kingdoms, before there was the written word, before there was religion, before lords and before there was paganism, one would find the Age of Alphas. In this early stage of mankind survival is paramount and tools are few. Man has left off living in caves and for some they have learned to build rudimentary structures (farmer/hunter) while others follow their herds (herder/hunter) from pasture land to pasture land. Survival for the farmer/hunter meant the same thing for the herder/hunter, a never ending struggle to obtain the basic four needs of life; water, food, shelter and companionship. It should also be noted that during this period safety from predators was only possible by fire, barricade or in numbers in defense. Regardless, the population of mankind was sufficient to guarantee their survival and survive they did.

In order for the species to propagate these isolated pockets of humanity would have to gather. There are only two times a year when a young population would want to interact collectively, in the mid to late spring and mid to late fall. The timing was accomplished by using the oldest clock known to man, the full moon. The fourth full moon after winter solace would time the spring gathering accurately. The eleventh full moon after winter solace would again time the gathering accurately. By mid to late spring the farmer/hunter would have survived the winter and would then have his seed in the ground. There would also be time to assess and recover from the damaging winter. A spring gathering at this point would be a welcome sight. For the herder/hunter the exercise would be the same. Assess the winter damage and prepare for the spring berthing. And again, the timing for a spring gathering would be welcome.

The spring gathering would be a time to exchange any residual surpluses and winter crafts for seed and stock. It would also be a time for available females to examine the available unattached males. The females would be looking for accomplished providers, even tempered and wholesome males while the males would be looking for accomplished cooks and care givers with an even temperament and wholesome. It was a sign of the times that the lame and unfortunate would never be selected for mating. It would never be the case of survival of the fittest but it would always be the case of survival of the best prepared. The elderly, lame and unfortunate would only survive so long as there were excess resources to permit such survival. By selecting a mate in the spring, the couple would have the bulk of the fair days of the year with which to establish their lives. There were no second chances in this period. The males would have to be prepared and both the males and females would have to choose wisely least the coming winter lay claim to them.

    The fall gathering at the eleventh full moon would be their last chance to exchange summer surpluses for seed and stock. It would also serve as a last opportunity to bid luck to each other as all strove to survive the coming winter.

*   Given that the physical capacities of the human being have not changed in a hundred thousand years, it becomes a moot point as to whether ancient man had the same abilities to rationalize and consider as does mankind today. The differences between those days and these are in the quantities of resources and technology.*

    Over time it would become obvious who were the masters at surviving from year to year. The healthiest and most long lived would be those with the greatest variety in their diet while those with restricted choices in their diet would die at a much earlier rate. The most successful survivors would then begin to assemble the lesser survivors and assign them specific task and all the while guaranteeing their survival. If the lesser survivors made it through the winter then the following year they would again accept whatever task was given them. And again, over time a settlement would be created with a single family as its head which in turn would dictate to the settlement members. The settlement would end the ordered Age of Alphas and chaos would be introduced into mankind.

    The Age of Alphas would vary, continent by continent, but the conduct of the age would remain consistent. An alpha male would choose his alpha female and both would begin life anew. Order into order until order fell into chaos.

Chuck Pyburn

An Essay on Order – Predestination

Ever since I could remember, I've always wondered how the right guys showed up at the right time to do the right thing. It was a perplexing quandary until I figured it out. With some hard work and introspection I came up with this essay.

The Essay

Predestination is the thought that, "I am here because I was meant to be here." If one considers the case of predestination then it must also be the case that an event has occurred wherein a single individual has claimed management of an event and its inevitable conclusion. To this end, when one considers order then one must consider the contributory factors of an event and logically conclude that the result of the event was mitigated by a participant that managed the contributory factors of the event.

If it were the case that choice had never been an issue from the birth of the event participant to the moment of the event then the case of predestination would have merit. However, it will always be the case that when those in proximity of an event see a void of indeterminate action then it will always be the case that one member of the event will take charge of the event. The remaining members of the event will comply as a choice preferable to letting the event dictate their reactions. Lastly, if an event is anticipated, then it will always be the case that those anticipating the event will invite the best available members of the population to consider the event prior to its occurrence. Furthermore, as with any event, the event will dictate that the most potentially successful member of the event will take charge of the actions to control the contributory factors of an event.

As with all events, there will be those who purposely engage themselves towards a potential event. One of the mainstays of order is preparedness. As one determines their preferred method of livelihood, they are then constantly engaged in bettering those skills that will move them forward in that field. Consequently, if or when an event occurs then this participatory member of the event has acquired the skills necessary to potentially manage the event to a successful conclusion.

If it is the case that an event occurs wherein there are no members of the event that can potentially manage the contributory factors of the event then the ensuing chaos of the event will continue until the contributory factors that cause the event have ceased their affects towards the event. In this case, the event will have exerted its maximum potential and achieved its most chaotic conclusion.

The final consideration of predestination is the purposeful event wherein an individual has purposely created an event so that they may singularly manage the event and thus claim predestination. In this case, the chaos of an event is considered to be acceptable collateral damage as nothing is more important than claiming predestination. As this event is engaged, those that are in order can only manage the resulting chaos as the event cannot be managed. Once the event has lost its momentum, then the one claiming predestination will claim ownership of controlling the event regardless of the effects of the event.

As the consternation of an event is injected between the concepts of order and chaos, there will always be those that claim predestination. The reality of an event is quite different in that ordered individuals will always do their utmost to either prevent an event or manage the contributory factors of an event. Predestination then becomes a chaotic title awarded to a single individual that unsuccessfully tried to manage an event that has already occurred since it will never be the case that one may claim predestination to an event that has not yet occurred.

Chuck Pyburn

An Essay on Order – Homeostasis, the Balance of Life

As a young kid I always wondered why people act and say the things they do. I even wondered why I act and say the things I do. I kept this wonder through two degrees and a lifetime of experience and still didn't have the answers. I didn't really understand until my second road trip to Sturgis and then it hit me, it's all about balance.

The Essay

Homeostasis is all about the body regulating itself, or to be more precise, it is all about the body trying to maintain order as we physically cause the body to be exposed to chaos. A person's physiology is constantly trying to fight off infections, fatigue, abuse, and any manner of exertions that a person will subject themselves to. This balance between what is taking place inside the body is in direct opposition to what is taking place outside of the body. More directly, what is being consumed by a body is then examined for value to the body before it is processed. If the body declares a consumed product to be good then it is converted to nutrients and if the body declares the consumption to be bad then it is physically discarded as quickly as possible. The mind of an individual undergoes a similar process as it moves from birth to death.

As the mind of individual matures it is constantly taking in new information. This process is achieved by the use of the five senses; touch, smell, taste, hearing and seeing. As in the manner of our physiology, if the mind determines the information to be good then it is processed as information worth knowing and consequently incorporating into our thought processes. If the information is determined to be bad then the mind will so class the information but only once, any similar occurrence in acquiring that information will be discarded since it has already been declared bad. Once the mind has processed enough good information then the mind will determine how best to use that information, hence personality, knowledge, capability and belief.

The most interesting aspect of this discussion is how the mind of an individual will maintain order regardless of the chaotic information it is introduced to. As an individual goes through their life their mind is constantly trying to balance the rational from the irrational and affecting the body to reflect those processes by action. Since it will always be the case that an individual cannot possibly do anything without the mind telling it to do so then it must be the case that the individual determined this action to be correct. It then must also be the case that an individual will continue this action until, when and only when, new or better information is acquired. The mind, upon learning new or better information, will then modify the body's response with regard to this new or better information, consequently a change in behavior.

It may also be the case that an individual has become comfortable with a thought process to the point of single-mindedness wherein, the person will reject new or better information so as to maintain the comfortable thought process. By so doing the individual is free to maintain a specific behavior without regard to external influences, whether the external influences are deemed good or bad.

Just as a person's body is in a constant struggle to maintain an ordered balance within so is that person's mind. The less chaos a body is exposed to then the healthier the body becomes; likewise, the less chaos the mind is exposed to then the healthier it becomes. If one were to expand the scope of this discussion to a population then the resulting conclusion would be equally applicable. The more order a population is exposed to then the healthier the population will be.

Chuck Pyburn

An Essay on Order – The Fallen Thought

Back in the old days of Special Forces there were three badges of honor. There were your military badges for successful missions and then there was your blue sapphire ring and your Rolex. Since I was only divorced once I only qualified for the blue sapphire. I never bought the ring but I certainly remember the thoughts around the divorce, even to this day. Those thoughts created this essay.

The Essay

The highest and most fragile of the ordered thoughts have three components; the thought, the emotions tied to the thought and the associations surrounding the thought. While all three components exist then so will the thought. If at any time one of the components fail then the thought will become chaos until either the emotional component or the associative component has been removed. Since it will never be the case that the thought can fail then it becomes the case that either the emotional or associative component must fail.

If it is the case that the emotional component has failed then it will be the case that those emotions that have been tied to the thought will have either been removed or replaced with either lesser emotions or no emotions. In either case, the thought will have fallen into chaos until such time as the physical things associated with the thought have been removed. By removing the things associated with the thought the individual may return the thought to order and move forward into other thought processes.

If it is the case that the associative component has failed then it will be the case that those physical things associated with the thought will have either been removed or replaced with either lesser associations or no associations. In either case, the thought will have fallen into chaos until such time as the emotions tied to the thought have been removed. By removing the emotions tied to the thought the individual may return the thought to order and move forward into other thought processes.

While the thought is complete then the rewards of the thought will have no bounds. If at any time the thought has fallen, then the ensuing chaos will equally have no bounds until such time as the thought is returned to order. For a thought to achieve this regard requires much time and effort and, likewise, for a fallen thought to be returned to order will also require much time and effort.

In this process there can be no shortcuts, the life of the highest and most fragile thought will exact its toll according to one's life. One's only saving grace will be the returning of the thought to order.

Chuck Pyburn

An Essay on Order – Friendship

I've never been much of a friend kind of person. As a kid I had one friend. As a teenager I had one friend. Throughout my military career I had one friend. I see a trend developing. The short answer is I didn't trust a whole lot of folks, the long answer is this essay.

The Essay

Friendship can only occur when it is the case, and only when it is the case, that two or more people are within proximity of each other and each are engaged in a singular, yet similar, task. It will then be the case that the participants will observe each other as they carry out their respective task. It will become obvious, over time, which participants are exceedingly good at their task and which are less than adequate at completing their task. The lesser qualified will engage the more qualified for assistance and the more qualified will engage the lesser qualified in hopes of demonstrating the skills necessary to accomplish their task.

As the two levels of participants engage, the lesser will engage the better in conversation to better ascertain various levels of equality in regards other than the task at hand. As targets of equality are determined, the lesser will attempt a bond with the better in hopes of maintaining a friendship until such time as the tasks are completed. The better may, or may not, remain engaged with the lesser until such time as the better has determined that the lesser is now qualified to complete their own task while the better completes theirs.

This friendship may continue after the tasks have been completed but will strictly be amiable or intermittent. If at any time the friendship escalates from amiable then it will always be the case that one friend will require the direct assistance of the other friend. In all cases this assistance will be with or without compensation and if there is compensation it will be less than the standard rates for such assistance if done by a professional. Once the need for assistance is no longer required then the friendship will return to its amiable or intermittent condition. This cycle of amiable to assistance to amiable will reoccur so long as the friendship last. When it becomes the case that assistance is withheld then the friendship at that is over.

There are of course other factors that can affect a friendship. If at any time during the friendship it becomes clear that only one participant is financing the assisted task then the friendship will dissolve. A second and more important factor in friendship is when it becomes clear that one participant in the friendship is attempting to usurp the wherewithal of the other participant without assuming the responsibilities of that wherewithal. In this condition the friendship will dissolve. And lastly, if it becomes evident, through the informality of the friendship, that one participant is attempting to inject themselves into the personal affairs of the other participant then the friendship will dissolve.

Within the business community, co-workers will only be friends so long as they are co-workers. Within the echelons of the work environment, juniors will attempt friendship with seniors but only so long as it may be advantageous. Friendliness within the work environment will only exist so long as those involved are paid and the friendly expectations are mandated. If at any time the conditions within the work environment change then so to will the expectation of friendliness change accordingly.

Within families friendship becomes a tertiary consideration as there are expectations as family above expectations as friends. The family as a unit will always have priority over the family as friends.

And lastly, the longevity of a friendship has a direct correlation to the equality of that friendship and only so long as those friend participants are in proximity to each other. Distance and time will always diminish a friendship as those participants move forward in their lives.

This essay does not characterize the aspects of friendship as in order or as in chaos. Friendship will in all cases be subjective to the individual and as such, each individual will have to determine for themselves the condition and quality of that friendship. It may be stated that since all people are drawn to other people that friendship is an ordered exercise; however, it will never be the case that one is required to be friends or that one be required to reciprocate to an invitation to be friends.

Chuck Pyburn

An Essay on Order – Rituals

In one of my few good childhood memories we had a Sunday ritual. Every Sunday morning mom would cook breakfast for the six of us, I had three brothers, and dad would put on a Johnny Cash album and then we would prepare for church. My recollection says this only happened for about three months but it was one of the better three months I can remember. When I considered that ritual along with all of the rituals I had to entertain in life I came up with this essay.

The Essay

In the days pre-dating the written language, rituals were used to pass down important information necessary for clan survival. These rituals were ordered events that occurred prior to major shifts in clan life. Inevitably there would be a single individual responsible for accurately leading the ritual as the clan participated. It would also be that individual's responsibility to train a replacement so that the ritual would continue as accurately as was taught to the ritual leader. As in all things human, individuals would embellish the ritual over time making the presentation of the ritual as grand an affair as the available resources would permit.

As the clan moved into a fledgling society, a spiritual aspect was developed and incorporated into the existing rituals of the clan. The ritual maintained order as it still provided the necessary guidance for a continuing society while at the same time recognizing the possibility of a supreme creator. This order was not interfered with until, at some point, the ritual leader claimed to interpret the intentions of the supreme creator. As these interpretations were subtle and introduced over time, they were nonetheless accepted by the population as necessary just as the rituals were accepted as necessary. These interpretations of the creator's intentions were the beginnings of chaos as an event in societal life.

These interpretations of the creator's intentions slowly developed into a religion that took advantage of the gathering requirement of the ritual. Over time the initial aspect of the ritual, information for survival, would be diminished as the society became ever more stable. As the initial requirement of the ritual diminished, the religious aspect of the ritual intensified until in the end, there would only be the religious aspect. And again, the rituals would be as grand an affair as resources would permit. The ritual had moved from an ordered event to a near totally chaotic event.

With the advent of the written language, the ritual in its form at the time would be carved in stone. The population would move from voluntary participation in the ritual to a mandated participation as the ritual gained dominance over the population. The ritual at this time became a totally chaotic event for the population from which there could be denying. Whatever activities the ritual demanded were seen as requirements from the creator and as such no personal blame or responsibility could be assigned to the ritual leaders as they were exempt by reason of faith in the ritual.

In all cases and in all societies where rituals had moved into total chaos, those societies have failed. It will never be the case that a ritual whose foundation is based in chaos will ever move those participants of that ritual forward. It is also the case that those societies that practiced rituals of total chaos would never again achieve dominance.

It then becomes clear that only those rituals that still maintain order, or a semblance of order, have survived over time. It is equally clear that the more chaos is introduced into an existing ritual then the more short lived that ritual will become until such time as that ritual will simply be denied participation.

Chuck Pyburn

An Essay on Order – The Classes

At the old age of twelve I was loading bread trucks at four in the morning when one of the owners told me that this job was probably the best I'd ever do. I only remember what he told me and my anger at knowing he was probably right. Folks from my side of town never amounted to much and I figured it might be set in stone. As I thought my way out of that hole I developed this essay.

The Essay

When one considers the classes of a population one should start with the commonality within a population and then develop the discussion into the various classes and why they exist. The three common aspects of all populations are birth, the four basic needs of life and death. While birth is necessarily a contributory engagement, there can never be a guarantee as to the condition of a child upon birth. Without argument, for whichever class the parents may belong to, it will have no affect on the condition of the child. With respect to the death commonality, belonging to a specific class may prolong life but regardless of class, death will in all cases claim the individual. With respect to the basic four needs of life which are water, food, shelter and companionship, all members of the population will seek these four needs relentlessly and again, without regard to class. Aside from the commonality, there are an ordered set of classes and then there are those classes that will represent chaos. It is also worth noting that in all cases of a population there have been, are, and will be classes within the population regardless of the category of the state.

Within the order of a population there is the class of position. It will always be the case that there will be those within a population that will assume a position that will place them in charge of a particular aspect of managing the population. For this position to be ordered it must be the case that the most qualified member of the population be selected. If the population member is not the most qualified then the position becomes the first class in chaos, status. Position then brings the discussion to the purpose of the class, responsibility.

As responsibility is the purpose of the class, it must be seen to with diligence and enthusiasm. If the responsibility aspect of the class is not conducted in an aggressive manner then the responsibilities to the population will not be met and the people will suffer the inadequacy. If the position is meant to achieve status then the population will most assuredly suffer the inadequacies as the responsibilities have no potential of being met.

After responsibilities comes the final aspect of the position class and that is replacement. An ordered member of the population will always consider their tenure in a position as temporary as they are aware of the final commonality within a population. A population member that entered the position to achieve status will never relinquish the position until mandated or until the final commonality has arrived. In the later case, the population will suffer the inadequacies of the position for that duration. In either case there will be a replacement and the only unknown aspect will be the qualifications of the replacement.

As positions are ever growing in their complexity and in the nature of their responsibilities, these basic principles will always apply. To achieve a position for the sake of status will always be at the costs of the population to be managed.

As with all positions, the greater the position the more segregation will be required between that member holding the position and the population. This segregation will allow that member holding the position to separate their basic four needs of life from the strains of the position. This segregation will also prevent unsolicited influence from minor sects within the population.

With regard to the chaotic member of the population attaining a position for status, this member will display a distinguishing lifestyle above the position and above the compensation derived from the position. This increase in income will be the direct result of misuse of the position for personal profit. As in all cases of positional status, once the position has again become vacant and then filled by a qualified individual, the memory of the predecessor will fade as will their acquisitions until nothing remains.

In not all cases does status equal chaos. There are those within the population that, through the conduct of business, acquire wealth and affluence. This wealth is acquired as the natural progression of providing goods and services to the population. This wealth is earned and consequently deserved and is in keeping with order. This attained wealth may be passed on to offspring, and then again to their offspring, until such time as the wealth no longer exist. In this regard, the individual may enjoy whatever affluence and status as may be derived. This particular status may only be construed as chaos if it is ever the case that the status causes harm to the population.

Within the population, to include those in positions to manage certain aspects of the population, there are two classes of members. The first member class within the population is those members that either have not secured their basic four needs of life or cannot secure those needs beyond threat. The second member class within the population is those members that have secured their basic four needs of life and have secured them beyond threat.

Throughout all populations there have been those members that have claimed a particular status within the population. This status will in all cases have been forced on the population by the guard of the individual claiming status. This particular status will only exist so long as the will to guard that status exist. When it becomes the case that the guard no longer has the will to enforce the status then again, the status will no longer exist and order has been restored.

Chuck Pyburn

An Essay on Order – Arming a Population

As you travel around the world you see how folks are treated by their local police and their country's military. You get a snapshot of what regular life must be like for the locals. The last party I attended in the Philippines was a pool side party and we had about fifteen armed guards with automatic weapons to ensure our safety. Granted this was about a hundred years ago but some memories stick.

The Essay

In the most general sense, a population should only need those weapons necessary to hunt worthy animals indigenous to that area wherein the population lives. And of those members of the population able to acquire weapons, only those that would actually hunt would need those weapons. The remainder of the population could reasonably be expected to live in peace and not require weapons; however, what is reasonable and what is reality is often very different.

The first precept of defense dictates that self defense and defense of one's family and property should only occur if it is the intention of the population member to maintain that measure of safety and to maintain that property in its current condition. This is not to say that, if in need, a population member could not cry out for assistance but it is to say that the assistance needed will never be there at the moment it is needed. Assistance will only occur after the threat has passed and the situation has moved from the chaos of threat to the order of assessment. If it is the case that the population member can reasonably contain the threat until assistance is offered then containment will be sufficient. If it is the case that containment is not a real possibility then the threat will have to be eliminated with sufficient force so as to return the situation to the point of safety or to where the population member's property is secure.

The second precept of defense dictates that the population should be armed so as to discourage the state from unilaterally compelling surrender of property or mandating servitude. The state will always have the option of enforcement of the state's will so long as the population has no wherewithal to compel grievance.

The third and final precept of defense dictates that a population should be armed so as to discourage a neighboring state from invasion. It will always be the case that as a prerequisite to war, a neighboring state will always consider the costs of war along with the costs of re-establishing the gained territorial infrastructure. If it is the case that the potential invaded territory is unarmed then the infrastructure will remain in tact as the war is conducted. If it is the case that the population is armed then the costs of the war will be protracted and the infrastructure will be destroyed. It will always be the case that when considering gains to losses that the invasion of a population will not occur or will not be sustained if the population is armed.

While weapons themselves are not a consideration of order, a discussion is nonetheless warranted if one is to be prepared for defense. A weapon can be construed as any object, of combination of objects, capable of carrying out the intended deadly force. If it is the case that the weapon is to be used for hunting then the population member need only acquire sufficient weaponry to dispatch the intended prey. If it is the case that the weapon will be used for self defense and safety then the weaponry should be superior to the weaponry that is anticipated in the execution of threat.

In all cases of defense and safety it should be noted that engagement is an all or nothing proposition. Other options for defense and safety are of course fleeing wherein the threat will consume those items for which it seeks. A final option for defense and safety would be to do nothing and allow the threat to occur at it's own pace. In this case the population member, and possibly the member's family, is at the mercy of the threat for so long as the threat will last or until assistance, if offered, has gained control of the threat.

The choices for the population and population member are few but lasting. The existence of threat to a member, or to a population, has been present since the days of tribes. The responses to threats have equally been present since the same number of days. One should choose their response to threat wisely as the call for order may only be made while one lives.

Chuck Pyburn

An Essay on Order – Acceptance

As a teenager, one of the hardest things I had to deal with was my parents divorcing. We never really had that much of a family anyway but it was still a blow. Within weeks after they broke up me and my three brothers pretty much went the way of the wind. Things could never be the same and that is what sparked this essay.

The Essay

One of the higher and more difficult aspects of order is acceptance. With regard to acceptance there can only be one of two conditions. It must either be the case that a person, place or thing is accepted by an individual, or by a population, or that an individual or population is accepted by a person, place or thing. It must also be the case that when there is acceptance that the condition of acceptance is 'as is' and in its totality and without modification.

Prior to acceptance is a realization that a specific condition exists to which an individual, or population, may, or may not, have contributed to or caused. Regardless of the cause of the specific condition, it does in fact exist and the individual, or population, is now engaged in the consequential affects of the specific condition. After realization comes understanding in that an individual, or population, becomes aware of their specific contributions, or involvement, as the outcome of the specific condition is achieved. While understanding defines participation it does not guarantee outcome.

When it is the case that a specific condition exists then it will also be the case that the specific condition will generate an outcome. It will also be the case that regardless of acceptance by an individual or population, that participation by an individual, or population, will be mandatory for the life of the specific condition.

Once it becomes the case that an individual, or population, realizes the existence of a specific condition and understands that they are a participant then it must be the case that any attempt to affect the outcome of the specific condition may only be achieved by accepting the specific condition. By accepting the specific condition in its totality an individual, or population, may begin an ordered process to mitigate the specific condition.

Acceptance then becomes a quiet resignation to the existence of a specific condition, an understanding of the participants of the specific condition, an awareness of the contributory factors of the specific condition and lastly, a process through which the specific condition will have the best possible outcome.

It should also be noted that the contributory elements that created the specific condition are at this point moot as the specific condition is in motion and an outcome will be generated. The worst possible outcome of any specific condition will be achieved when the chaos of a specific condition is allowed to dictate its participants and terms of existence. Through the order of acceptance one may determine how quickly one may exert control over a given condition and determine who may participate. Order will further determine how one may impact the life of the condition and the subsequent outcome.

There will always be the presence of specific conditions and these conditions will always be the direct result of human interaction. And it will always be the case that only those individuals, or populations, that accept the specific conditions may influence those conditions.

Chuck Pyburn

An Essay on Order – Melancholy

Like anybody else, you just can't get through life without some ups and downs. Unfortunately, as a kid I kind of anticipated more ups than downs and as usual, life told me I wasn't getting away that easy. There worst for me so far was not being invited to either of my parent's funerals. These two non-events really sent me on a spiral which brings me to this essay.

The Essay

Throughout the course of every individual's life there will be challenges that exceed one's ability to comprehend. When it is the case that these life challenges are based on the good aspects of life the individual will experience heightened elation which will last until the individual has been able to absorb the moment. When it is the case that these life challenges are based on the bad aspects of life the individual will experience depression which will last until the individual has been able to absorb the moment. Each of these emotional extremes follows the confines of order just as the life challenge follows the confines of order.

A life challenge will only fall into chaos if the participants of the life challenge fall into chaos. A participant will exhibit chaotic behavior if it is the case that the participant fails to mange their own emotional contributions to the event or fails to manage their specific involvement of the event. In either case, the responsibility of managing that particular aspect will fall to another individual with no guarantee of outcome. The event will remain in chaos until it is the case that the individual's emotional and participatory aspects have been satisfactorily resolved.

When it is the case that one is involved with a life challenge based on the good aspects of life and one enjoys the subsequent feelings of elation that there will be a corresponding surge of adrenaline to sustain that emotion. For the remainder of the event to not fall into chaos will be determined by how quickly the individual can regain their composure and allow the adrenaline surge to subside.

When it is the case that one is involved with a life challenge based on the bad aspects of life then it will be the case that one will have the emotion of depression. A depressive state will be determined by one's own ability to cope with the negative aspects of the life challenge and may range from melancholy to clinical. For the remainder of the event to not fall into chaos will be determined by how quickly the individual can recover from their depression and return to a normal attitude.

As life challenges will occur and reoccur for the life of an individual it becomes prerequisite upon the individual to anticipate these events and their responses. And as not all life challenges may be anticipated, it becomes crucial that an individual be emotionally flexible in that they are able to reconcile the event personally and mange their contributory efforts towards the event less the event and the individual fall into chaos.

Maintaining emotional stability is no less difficult than maintaining order, each requires daily evaluation and effort. Towards this effort one should consider that order is that which allows the individual to move forward in their life.

Chuck Pyburn

An Essay on Order – Proof

I remember as a small child when my grandmother accused me of stealing her bus money. Back in those days your choices of getting to work were the county bus or walking, we were to far out for local taxis. Grandma couldn't find her money in the kitchen and I took one of the worst beatings of my life. On her way out the door to catch the bus she found her money on a small table next to the front door.

The Essay

Proof is a stand alone word used to convey the existence of an event, person, or material object either in the past or in near real-time. Proof can never be used in real-time as the event, person or material object does exist and is engaged. Proof is only of value to the current population and proof is only considered factual at the time the proof is offered. Proof offered in the past requires current validation to again be considered as proof. Proof is subjective in that only those elements of existence required to substantiate the claim are gathered as facts that then make the case of proof. Proof, or the lack of proof, then becomes one of the more abstract elements of order. Proof becomes abstract when it is used as a basis for considerations in regard to the validity of an event, person or material object. Each of these bases will be examined for their need of proof and what that proof will offer.

An event is perhaps the most difficult of proofs as it pertains strictly to cause and effect. One must be able to substantiate the elements of cause before one can postulate a specific occurrence and then substantiate that the subsequent effects occurred only as the result of the specific occurrence. As all of the elements of cause and all of the elements of effect may never be acquired, proof in regard to an event becomes reasonable inference in that the event did occur based on the quality of information gathered. If the information gathered is not factually quantitative then the proof fails and the event is denied. If the event is proven then it may be offered to the population as proven and the event is in order. The event will then remain in order until such time as the population demands that the event be re-validated and again proven. If the event is denied but offered to the population as proven then the event will reflect chaos and all the members of the population that accept the event will retain that chaotic acceptance. In this case the chaos will be retained until the event is re-validated and proof is again denied and the proof is offered to the population as denied and subsequently accepted by the population as denied. Chaos in this case will be restored to order.

With regard to proof of a person the proof becomes somewhat limited. Proof that a person did exist is limited to physical evidence and lineage. Recollection and being named within a document may offer reasonable inference but only physical evidence or traceable lineage will offer proof. Proof of the existence of a person will become more exasperated based on the importance of the person within the population. If it is the case that the existence is proven then order will prevail until such time as the population requires that the proof be re-validated. If it is the case that the proof is denied and the denial is accepted by the population then again, order has prevailed and the population will move forward and the proof will never again be required. If it is the case that the proof is denied but reasonable inference is accepted by the population then an element of chaos has been introduced into the population. This chaos will remain with the population until such time as the reasonable inference is denied by the population or until such time as physical evidence or lineage has been proven.

When one considers the proof of a material object then one must conclude that the material object did so exist prior to the proof of the existence and will so exist regardless if having been proved to exist. As the population manipulates material objects to better serve the population, each of the manipulations must be a proven betterment prior to being accepted by the population. If the manipulation is not a proven betterment then it will be discarded by the population. It will also be the case that each time the manipulation is used that it again is proving its betterment. When it is the case that a manipulation fails then it will be discarded and replaced with a similar or better manipulation. Proof of the existence of the material object then only becomes necessary if it is the case that the material object is going to be a contributory element to a manipulation. It will also be the case that all manipulations will, over time, return to the original condition of the material object. Proof of the existence of a material object is also in keeping with order as it expands knowledge and awareness.

Chuck Pyburn

An Essay on Order – Power and the Population

Having crossed the North Atlantic in the winter time you get to see first hand the power of nature and the power of man. A heavy cruiser is no small boat and to be tossed around like a feather in the wind was most impressive. In fact, I'd been at sea for seven months prior to this crossing and it was the first time I heaved my guts and it was totally embarrassing.

The Essay

In real terms power is moving mass distance. When one regards the population and power the principles are essentially the same while the applications differ in how power is applied. The elements that comprise a power great enough to affect a population are authority, responsibility, argument, enforcement, benefit and consequence. As in all endeavors regarding power, the amount of time required to affect a population to a final attitude in regards to a specific application of power is not relevant as the power applied will be relentless until achieved.

As in all populations authority within the population is pyramidal in that there will be leader positions of small groups and then the leader positions of the small group leaders until finally there is a pinnacle authority. Therefore, in all cases of population, there will be a final pinnacle position wherein the authority to direct the population exists.

While the pinnacle position will have the responsibility of the success or failure of applied power it does not bear the consequence of failure nor does it directly enjoy the benefits of applied power. The population will in all cases enjoy the affects of the applied power while the pinnacle position will enjoy the final responsibility of the applied power, in that it either brought order or that it brought chaos.

The pinnacle position will make the final argument in regards to, is the power applied or is it not applied. Those leader positions below the pinnacle position will defend the argument so long as the population deems it favorably. If it is the case that the population declines the argument and subsequently cannot be coerced then the lesser leader positions will decline the argument as well. If it is the case that the pinnacle position's argument is declined then the pinnacle position will wait for a more favorable time to make the argument as time is not a factor.

As populations are always slow to move towards a new attitude, enforcement becomes the tool of choice to achieve momentum over inertia. The pinnacle position will apply the greatest use of enforcement and then those lesser leader positions will apply their available enforcement measures in an equal effort to comply. The enforcement will be directed at those members of the population that are resisting the new attitude as well as those members that are moving to far into order or too far into chaos. The residual population unable to adopt the new attitude will be considered an acceptable loss as the bulk of the population is at rest in the new attitude.

    The benefit achieved by the applied power may only be determined after the power has been applied and the population is at rest. The benefit to the population now in the new attitude will only be short lived. While a population may exist in a specific geographical location it is nonetheless constantly in motion just as its needs are constantly in motion. A specific benefit from a specific application of power will only last until the population moves passed it and then the benefit will no longer exist. Regardless of the effects of the new attitude the pinnacle position will have achieved its objective and the benefit is now enjoyed by the population.

    The consequences of the new attitude are irreversible in that the population may never return to a previous attitude. Thus the consequences of applied power are such that they evolve a population into a rightful place in world dominance. Those applications of power that move a population closer to order enjoy greater presence while those applications of power that move a population towards chaos will enjoy less presence.

Chuck Pyburn

An Essay on Order – Poverty

Poverty is one of those things you can find in any country at just about any time in history. Once I was old enough to know that I lived in poverty I promised myself it was a one-way street out of there. The why of poverty evaded me for a long time but I finally came up with an answer.

The Essay

Poverty is the human condition wherein, regardless of ability, an individual is unable to secure the four basic needs of life on a daily basis. *The four basic needs of life are water, food, shelter and companionship.* The cause of this inability is as relevant as the condition itself. Of the cause of poverty there can be only one answer, the ruling authority. For an individual to continue a life in poverty there can be only one reason, choice. Regardless of cause and condition, while an individual is living in poverty they are not a productive member of the population and as such will not be accepted as equals by the population nor will they be able to evolve as the population moves forward. It is also worth noting that wealth can never be a causal factor in regards to poverty as wealth may only be acquired by providing goods or services to the population at the discretion of the ruling authority.

When it is the case that a ruling authority leaves off administering for a population and begins caring for a population then it will always be the case that the ruling authority will promote poverty over responsibility. Inversely, when it is the case that a ruling authority, through laws and regulations, deprives a population of the wherewithal to acquire the four basic needs of life then the ruling authority will have caused an impoverished condition within the population. In either case, those members of the population that are living in poverty will lack the wherewithal to singularly enjoy the benefits of acquiring the basic four needs of life.

When it is the case that an individual does live in poverty then the choices become as limited as the available resources. One may resign one's self to a life of poverty and eke out whatever existence may be possible or one could abandon the impoverished environment is search of a more conducive environment where that ruling authority does not impose poverty. It should also be noted that while one lives in poverty one is at the mercy of the ebb and flow of poverty in that one cannot determine the direction one wishes their life to follow.

If it is the case that those members of the population living in poverty have determined to wait for the current ruling authority to expire in hopes that a more ordered ruling authority will take its place then they are committed to a life of poverty. A ruling authority will only reverse itself when it is the case that the population is in rebellion. It has always been the case that when poverty exists within the confines of a ruling authority that the condition of poverty will in time overtake a population, a condition that will not endure. A population cannot strive in the chaos of poverty.

Chuck Pyburn

An Essay on Order – Dominance

Back in my younger and seriously more stupid days, I rode with a bike gang that was pretty much less than a pleasant bunch of guys. The president of the chapter was a guy I had known from childhood so acceptance of my participation was without question. It was not so much that my friend was a good leader but more the case that he had dominance. If things didn't go his way he'd take your head off, give you a beating or both. Watching my buddy gave me pause to reflect on how this action played out on a larger scale and that thought became this essay.

The Essay

Dominance, in all cases, is the thoughtful and congruent application of chaos. It is thoughtful in that it is applied with intention and with callous disregard. It is congruent in that there may only be dominance when there are adequate resources that support the domination. Dominance, and again in all cases, will only be disqualified as an authority when it is the case that one, or all, of the supporting resources has been eliminated. Dominance may only exist outside of jurisprudence as the dominant entity provides its own application of equality. The enemy of dominance is of course order, and as order may never be stifled, dominance will never stand as an authority over time. There are three levels of equality within dominance; there are those that are dominated, those that support the domination and finally, the entity that incurred the dominance.

With regard to those that are dominated, it will always be the case that the dominant may deprive those dominated of one, or all, of their basic four needs of life. *The basic four needs of life are water, food, shelter and companionship.* It then becomes the case that the dominated will comply with the domination as a simple matter of survival until such time as the domination ends. It will also be the case that there will be a sect of the dominated engaged in a constant struggle to eliminate the weakest resource of the domination. This sect will be relentless in that living in chaos will offer no alternative.

As for the resources of the dominant, the resources will support the domination as a result of immediate reward for that support. So long as the dominant entity provides such reward the support will continue. If it is ever the case that the dominant entity fails to provide such reward then it will also be the case that the resource will fail in its provision and look elsewhere for its reward. When it does become the case that a resource fails in its provision then it will also be the case that the domination will become short lived and order will be restored.

The dominant entity will only regard itself and its immediate members as equal, all other factions are regarded in accordance with their specific contributions to the domination. The dominant entity will maintain its posture so long as the dominated are in compliance and the resources permit. When it does become the case that domination will no longer be sustained then it will always be the case that the dominant entity will look to escape and reestablishment in a more conducive environment. The dominant entity will never look to itself as a failing authority and will always regard the dominated as the benefactors of a superior intellect.

Dominance has always been a plague to mankind. The consideration that a few may direct the many and that the many must respond as directed. Order does not dictate that you will, order dictates that you may. Order does not respond to a single choice but will respond to the choices that are available. The attitude of dominance is an attitude of chaos, an attitude of tolerance and assistance is an attitude of order.

Chuck Pyburn

An Essay on Order – Reckoning

Towards the end of my teenage years I got to spend a little over a year with my aunt and uncle, the idea was for me to finish High School. It wasn't that I was rescued but more the case that I thought that if I had a little help I could pull it off. About halfway through my junior year it all went south and I was thrown back into the mix of society. I did take advantage of my one normal year to take stock of where I was and where I was going. That bit of insight planted the seed that has grown into this essay.

The Essay

Reckoning is a method used in navigation to determining one's position in time and space and in so doing allows and individual to navigate from a point of origin to a point of destination. With regard to self-evaluation, reckoning allows an individual to understand their origins, their current position and then finally, their future as they determine it. While the process of self-evaluation is an ordered process it does not preclude an individual from the effects of chaos either before the self-evaluation or after, each individual must dictate their own course.

When reckoning the past it is worth noting the processes that occurred to allow an individual to be present in this time and space. As an individual does exist it must then be the case that their contributing parents do, or did, also exists. And because an individual does exist it must then be the case that their lineage could be traced back to the point of origins. One should remember that as history unfolded it self there would be occasions where an entire family, or families, would be terminated. These occasions of termination would result in their lineage also being terminated. Those terminated families could no longer offer offspring to propagate the species. The inevitable conclusion is that those ancestors that did contribute to an individual's existence did survive war, disease, famine and catastrophe. When one considers that, over time, there were hundreds and thousands of single individuals with each making their best possible selection for mating and that all of that time and effort went into producing what stands in the mirror today, it is quite the thought. Also in this process was the thought that each generation was working to make a better generation until finally this generation is in control of the destiny of mankind. When one reckons the past one should not just reckon the immediate past but should include the many, many, generations that came before the immediate past. In the final analysis, an individual exist today because countless hundreds of individuals survived and contributed to make the single an unique individual that does exist today. This existence is in order, what may or may not be in order is what that individual does with the existence.

When one reckons their existence today one should first be aware of the quantity and quality of actual time that is in consideration. When it is the case that the quantity of time is being considered then one should consider the date of birth as the only known factor. While it is true that an individual may enjoy an extremely long life, it is also true that an individual will expire from either natural or man-made causes. It then becomes the case that since the time of expiration remains an unknown as far as quantity, it does become a known in that it will occur. Consequently, the only guarantees one may assume is in the existence one is currently enjoying. Reckoning in quantity of time then becomes the regard an individual places on order and quality of existence in the now and near term while anticipating an extended existence beyond the near term. And lastly, it then becomes the case that the only existence one may enjoy beyond expiration is through their offspring.

As one reckons the future one should be aware that they will not share an existence into that future. Each individual may only exist in current time and as such may never participate in future events. There are only two aspects on an individual that may exist in the future, their contributions to the population and their memories as realized by those individuals that had familiarity. All other aspects of an individual, real or tertiary, will be distributed within the family or returned to the population.

As one reckons their existence one should be keenly aware of the dynamics of that existence. The rules of existence are very straightforward and easily understood but extremely difficult to grasp. When it becomes the case that one understands their position in time, and their limits on that time, then one may begin to plot their course to their final destination. While the point of origin and the point of final destination are ordered, only the individual may determine their course through existence.

Chuck Pyburn

An Essay on Order – Change

As I make it through this life of mine, one of the hardest things I've had to deal with is change. And of those changes the one that is upon me now is old age. Getting old is a tough one but as the saying goes, when you only have two choices, getting old is definitely preferable. Change is still something that needs to be addressed and I thought I'd write this essay.

The Essay

Change is the direct result of the motion of life, whether in regards to an individual or to a population. The implication, therefore, becomes the case that so long as there is the motion of life there will be change and that without life, change is no longer relevant. As change is an ordered event, one should anticipate that change will occur and that as one engages in the motion of life, the act of engagement will result in a change. With regards to an individual, or population, there can be only two attitudes as the change occurs, resistance or acceptance. One should also note that, regardless of the attitude, change will occur, and will continue to occur, so long as there is life.

When it becomes the case that there is resistance to change then it will also be the case that the individual, or population, will become stagnant and segregated from those that have accepted the change and have adapted. When resistance to change becomes resolute then it will always be the case that the resulting chaos of the resistance will disallow participation with those that have accepted the change. It will always be the case that those that do resist change will envision a pre-change environment as preferable to a post-change environment and will endeavor to re-establish the pre-change environment. While a pre-change environment may be examined it will never be the case that a change can be undone. The motion of life moves in one direction only and as such, an individual, or population, must accept the inevitability of change lest they loose their ability to participate, in real time, with the population that has accepted the change.

As change does occur, it then becomes the contest of the rightness of a change. The determination of rightness is assessed by examining the conditions that incurred the change. Notwithstanding the conditions, the change has occurred and the subsequent condition does exist. It then becomes incumbent on the individual, or population, to bring order into the post change environment. If it becomes the case that the individual, or population, fails to establish order then the change will continue to occur until such time as order is established. When and only when, order is established in a post-change environment does the rightness of change then become apparent.

Chuck Pyburn

An Essay on Order – Peace

One of things I enjoy most is fishing. To me there is nothing like being out on the lake, on my boat of course, with no hearing aids and not a person in sight. I don't have to talk to anyone or listen to anyone. I'm free to ponder anything and everything and maybe catch a few fish in the process and yes I do catch and release. For a few hours I'm at peace with myself and the world is a good place to be. One of the things I ponder is peace and this is the essay.

The Essay

Peace is not the absence of war; it is the absence of violent conflict. Conflict may only occur when it is the case that there are two or more parties in such disagreement that only violence may resolve the disagreement. It then becomes the case that only two entities have the wherewithal to escalate a conflict to violence between populations; religion and the ruling authority.

As in all cases of religion, there is the pervading understanding that theirs is the only real and correct doctrine and that all other doctrines must be false. It then becomes the case that a conversion is warranted on all those that do not accept the one doctrine as the most correct. This intolerance of belief will result in the chaos of force against those of other beliefs. In all cases, when it becomes the condition that those of a particular belief condescend to violence that the order of peace will not exist. It will also be the case that when the last 'non-believer' has been converted that religion will no longer exist.

When it becomes the case that a ruling authority has determined to violently engage a neighboring population then it will always be the case that the ruling authority will be short lived. It will never be the case that a population, of their own accord, will violently engage a neighboring population. The invaded population will contest this violation by any and all means available and until such time as their sovereignty has been restored.

Peace, and more rightly the order of peace, is never difficult to accomplish so long as there is tolerance and a justly administering ruling authority. It will never be the case that peace will coexist with the single-minded control of a ruling authority or the belligerence of a mandated doctrine.

Chuck Pyburn

An Essay on Order – The Final Essay

I've had a great time writing these essays and like everything else, all things must come to an end. If you have managed to hang tough for the first seventy-nine, I hope you can hang for this last one. Best wishes and long life, enjoy the essay.

The Essay

We learn from history that we learn nothing from history as history continues to repeat itself. With each generation there is the thought that what happened then will not happen now, even as it is happening. There is not one master stroke that can break this cycle of chaos but it does exist within each individual. As one individual leaves off the shackles of chaos and enters into the realm of order so to will there be another. Order is relentless in its pursuit of equality and freedom, tolerance and justice, choice and fulfillment. Chaos will only prevail over the weak-minded and ignorant. The greatest single statement any one individual may declare is, "I choose".

Chuck Pyburn